WOMEN
AND
WORK
IN THE NEW TESTAMENT

THEOLOGY OF WORK   PROJECT

WOMEN
AND
WORK
IN THE NEW TESTAMENT

THE BIBLE AND YOUR WORK
Study Series

HENDRICKSON
PUBLISHERS

**Theology of Work, The Bible and Your Work Study Series:
Women and Work in the New Testament**

ISBN 978-1-61970-824-2

William Messenger, Executive Editor, Theology of Work Project
Sean McDonough, Biblical Editor, Theology of Work Project
Patricia Anders, Editorial Director, Hendrickson Publishers

Contributor:
Alice Mathews, "Women and Work in the New Testament" Bible Study

The Theology of Work Project is an independent, international organization
dedicated to researching, writing, and distributing materials with a biblical
perspective on work. The Project's primary mission is to produce resources
covering every book of the Bible plus major topics in today's workplaces.
Wherever possible, the Project collaborates with other faith-and-work or-
ganizations, churches, universities and seminaries to help equip people for
meaningful, productive work of every kind.

Printed in the United States of America

First Printing—July 2016

Contents

The Theology of Work

Work is not only a human calling, but also a divine one. "In the beginning God created the heavens and the earth." God worked to create us and created us to work. "The LORD God took the man and put him in the garden of Eden to till it and keep it" (Gen. 2:15). God also created work to be good, even if it's hard to see in a fallen world. To this day, God calls us to work to support ourselves and to serve others (Eph. 4:28).

Work can accomplish many of God's purposes for our lives—the basic necessities of food and shelter, as well as a sense of fulfillment and joy. Our work can create ways to help people thrive; it can discover the depths of God's creation; and it can bring us into wonderful relationships with co-workers and those who benefit from our work (customers, clients, patients, and so forth).

Yet many people face drudgery, boredom, or exploitation at work. We have bad bosses, hostile relationships, and unfriendly work environments. Our work seems useless, unappreciated, faulty, frustrating. We don't get paid enough. We get stuck in dead-end jobs or laid off or fired. We fail. Our skills become obsolete. It's a struggle just to make ends meet. But how can this be if God created work to be good—and what can we do about it? God's answers for these questions must be somewhere in the Bible, but where?

The Theology of Work Project's mission has been to study what the Bible says about work and to develop resources to apply the

Christian faith to our work. It turns out that every book of the Bible gives practical, relevant guidance that can help us do our jobs better, improve our relationships at work, support ourselves, serve others more effectively, and find meaning and value in our work. The Bible shows us how to live all of life—including work—in Christ. Only in Jesus can we and our work be transformed to become the blessing it was always meant to be.

To put it another way, if we are not following Christ during the 100,000 hours of our lives that we spend at work, are we really following Christ? Our lives are more than just one day a week at church. The fact is that God cares about our life *every day of the week*. But how do we become equipped to follow Jesus at work? In the same ways we become equipped for every aspect of life in Christ—listening to sermons, modeling our lives on others' examples, praying for God's guidance, and most of all by studying the Bible and putting it into practice.

This Theology of Work series contains a variety of books to help you apply the Scriptures and Christian faith to your work. This Bible study is one volume in the series The Bible and Your Work. It is intended for those who want to explore what the Bible says about work and how to apply it to their work in positive, practical ways. Although it can be used for individual study, Bible study is especially effective with a group of people committed to practicing what they read in Scripture. In this way, we gain from one another's perspectives and are encouraged to actually *do* what we read in Scripture. Because of the direct focus on work, The Bible and Your Work studies are especially suited for Bible studies *at* work or *with* other people in similar occupations. The following lessons are designed for thirty-minute lunch breaks (or perhaps breakfast before work) during a five-day work week.

Christians today recognize God's calling to us in and through our work—for ourselves and for those whom we serve. May God use this book to help you follow Christ in every sphere of life and work.

Will Messenger, Executive Editor
Theology of Work Project

Introduction

People everywhere have always worked. Fans of television series such as *Downton Abbey* may envy a "leisure class" with nothing more to do than drink tea and visit others in the leisure class, but even there key persons must "work."

So what constitutes *work*? Is work only what we do for some kind of remuneration? Does that "remuneration" have to be cash, or can it be the pleasure we take in any job well done? Or is it anything we do to sustain our lives or the lives of others, with or without a paycheck? A homemaker without a paycheck may well put in as many hours in her home (her "workplace") as someone in an office or factory, working from nine to five o'clock, five days a week. The bottom line is that people everywhere have always worked.

When we turn to the first chapter of the Bible, we watch God "at work" creating our cosmos and a world in which human beings can survive, even thrive. The second chapter begins by telling us, "Thus the heavens and the earth were finished, and all their multitude. And on the seventh day God finished the *work* that he had done, and he rested on the seventh day from all the *work* that he had done" (Gen. 2:1–2; emphasis added).

We may think of the Garden of Eden as some kind of leisure vacation setting, but God placed the first man and woman in that garden to work together, tilling it and caring for it (Gen. 2:15, 18). Anyone who gardens knows that it takes constant work to maintain one, even in Eden. So from the beginning of time and throughout the Bible we see people at work, many simply to survive. Thus it comes as no surprise that women throughout the ages have always worked, often alongside men, sometimes alone, but in harmony with the work that men were doing.

When we turn to the New Testament, there we also find women engaged in all kinds of work. For some it was the work of bearing and rearing children. For others it was bringing aid to folks in need. For still others it was as businesswomen engaged in profitable enterprises. And for many it was in some form of ministry for Christ and his kingdom. As you work through this study of women at work two thousand years ago in the Middle East, you'll find that while our lives today are radically different, some things never change. In many cases their issues are still issues for us today. How they handled their work life may help us in managing ours in ways that bring honor to God and joy to us in the midst of our work.

Chapter 1

The Three Wise Women of Christmas

Lesson #1: The First Wise Woman—Mary, the Mother of Jesus (Luke 1:26–56)

Most of us grew up hearing about the "three wise men," in the Christmas story, even singing the carol "We Three Kings." As adults, we know that the Bible doesn't actually tell us how *many* wise men or *magi* followed the star from the East to Bethlehem. There may have been three or nine or even fifteen, for all we know. We *do* know, however, about three wise *women* in the Christmas story. We meet them in Luke 1 and 2.

A young girl named Mary, wise beyond her years, lived in the town of Nazareth. In her culture, marriages were arranged for very young girls and weddings took place soon after a young woman began menstruating. Mary was in her early teens and was engaged to marry an older man, a local carpenter named Joseph. He was established in the town and would be able to support the family God would give them.

One day, as Mary pondered her future life as Joseph's wife, suddenly the room was filled with a mighty presence, God's angel Gabriel. Can you imagine her reaction when she heard the angelic voice speak "Greetings, favored one! The Lord is with you" (Luke 1:28)? How would you have reacted had that happened to you?

As Mary tried to sort out her feelings about that greeting, the angel continued:

> "Do not be afraid, Mary, for you have found favor with God. And now, you will conceive in your womb and bear a son, and you will name him Jesus. He will be great, and will be called the Son of the Most High, and the Lord God will give to him the throne of his ancestor David. He will reign over the house of Jacob forever, and of his kingdom there will be no end." (Luke 1:30–33)

What? Could this be happening? Gabriel was talking about God's promised Messiah, and Mary was to bring that baby into the world! Timidly she asked, "How can this be, since I am a virgin?" She had hardly framed the question before Gabriel answered it:

> "The Holy Spirit will come upon you, and the power of the Most High will overshadow you; therefore the child to be born will be holy; he will be called Son of God. And now, your relative Elizabeth in her old age has also conceived a son; and this is the sixth month for her who was said to be barren. For nothing will be impossible with God." (Luke 1:34–37)

Mary's immediate response was "Here am I, the servant of the Lord; let it be with me according to your word" (Luke 1:38). As suddenly as it had come, the mighty presence left the room and Mary was alone to think about what had just happened. She knew that virtually every woman in her country dreamed of becoming the mother of God's Messiah. Perhaps she had only dreamed this herself. Had she really had a visit from God's angel Gabriel?

Then she remembered the words of Gabriel said about her relative, Elizabeth. If what the angel had said about barren Elizabeth was true, then this was no dream! She would make the long journey from Galilee down to Judea to see for herself.

We may not think of Mary's motherhood as "work," but in declaring herself the servant of the Lord, she became a partner in God's work to invade a broken and sinful world and reverse the grip of evil on people's lives. There would be physical work in bearing and rearing this special child, to be sure. But partnership with God would involve her in a much larger picture. She captured some of that in the song she sang:

> "My soul magnifies the Lord, and my spirit rejoices in God my Savior, for he has looked with favor on the lowliness of his servant. . . . He has shown strength with his arm; he has scattered the proud in the thoughts of their hearts. He has brought down the powerful from their thrones, and lifted up the lowly; he has filled the hungry with good things, and sent the rich away empty." (Luke 1:46–48a, 51–53)

Mary knew that God casts down the proud and lifts up the lowly. Her work of bearing and rearing God's Messiah would lead to the great reversal, the ultimate redemption of our sin-soaked world.

 Food for Thought

As you think about your sphere of work, whatever it is, how do you see God using you as an agent of change for good where you are?

_____

_____

_____

_____

_____

_____

_____

_____

If you think about yourself as being in partnership with God, what could that change about how you view yourself and the work you do?

_____

_____

_____

_____

_____

_____

_____

_____

Lesson #2: The Second Wise Woman—Elizabeth (Luke 1:1–25, 57–80)

In the ancient Near East, a woman's most important function was to bear sons for her husband. Nothing else came close to that in importance. So when a woman was barren, it carried a stigma she had to live with throughout her adult life. Mary's cousin Elizabeth, now an old woman long postmenopausal, lived with that curse year in and year out. Then came the angelic word to her husband, Zechariah, that in her old age she would give birth to a son (Luke 1:13). This was a first-order miracle, no doubt about it.

Can you see the hand of God in this? God was already at work through the five-months-pregnant Elizabeth at the time the angel Gabriel appeared to Mary. We may think that God works only in our own small corner without realizing that the Master Chess Player in the universe is never doing only one thing at a time, but has multiple players on the world-board moving toward grand purposes. Mary up in Galilee needed time with her relative Elizabeth down in Judea as both faced miraculous pregnancies.

Luke tells us what happened when Mary finally arrived at Elizabeth's door:

> [Mary] entered the house of Zechariah and greeted Elizabeth. When Elizabeth heard Mary's greeting, the child leaped in her womb. And Elizabeth was filled with the Holy Spirit and exclaimed with a loud cry, "Blessed are you among women, and blessed is the fruit of your womb. And why has this happened to me, that the mother of my Lord comes to me? For as soon as I heard the sound of your greeting, the child in my womb leaped for joy. And blessed is she who believed that there would be a fulfillment of what was spoken to her by the Lord." (Luke 1:40–45)

Elizabeth's surprising confirmation of Mary's pregnancy affirmed the angel Gabriel's message: This lowly peasant girl from Nazareth would, in fact, bring God's Messiah into the world. She had not merely dreamed a dream. She was living a new reality as the mother of God's Son.

How did Elizabeth know what to say as Mary entered her house? It was a direct revelation from God's Spirit. These two women of little or no account in their culture were instruments of God's hands in a world-changing work. Elizabeth's son (John the Baptist) would be the last of the great Old Testament prophets, foretold by Isaiah: "A voice cries out, 'In the wilderness prepare the way of the LORD, make straight in the desert a highway for our God'" (Isa. 40:3). Mary's son, Jesus, would make possible a new relationship with God through his death and resurrection. John was the forerunner and Jesus the Savior.

We sometimes think that because we're not rich or famous, we can't possibly play a major role in what God is doing in the world.

But the Bible turns that idea on its head. The Apostle Paul captured this in his first letter to the Christians at Corinth:

> But God chose what is foolish in the world to shame the wise; God chose what is weak in the world to shame the strong; God chose what is low and despised in the world, things that are not, to reduce to nothing things that are, so that no one might boast in the presence of God. (1 Cor. 1:27–29)

A teenage girl from the backwater town of Nazareth in northern Palestine and the aged wife of an ordinary priest living as a peasant in the highlands of Judea: both stood amazed that God indeed uses the weak of this world to confound the mighty. We can never assume that we're too insignificant to be used by God, perhaps in some surprising ways. Instead, we can choose to partner with God in his work of redeeming a broken world.

 Food for Thought

What are some lessons you can glean from the ways Mary and Elizabeth accepted their calling from God?

_____

_____

_____

_____

_____

_____

_____

Regardless of your position, what might be some ways in which God can work through you in your workplace?

_____

_____

_____

_____

_____

_____

Lesson #3: The Third Wise Woman—The Prophet Anna (Luke 2:22–40)

Birth customs differ from age to age and from country to country. In first-century Palestine when a woman gave birth, she was considered "unclean" as long as the postpartum bleeding continued. She could not touch anything sacred. But on the fortieth day after giving birth, she could be "purified" from the bleeding by taking an offering to the temple in Jerusalem. At the same time her baby would be presented to the Lord:

> When the time came for their purification according to the law of Moses, [Mary and Joseph] brought [baby Jesus] up to Jerusalem to present him to the Lord (as it is written in the law of the Lord, "Every firstborn male shall be designated as holy to the Lord"), and they offered a sacrifice according to what is stated in the law of the Lord, "a pair of turtledoves or two young pigeons." (Luke 2:22–24)

We watch this couple push their way through the crowded streets of the city with their offering, carrying a baby now nearly six weeks old. Reaching the temple steps, they are interrupted twice by old people.

First, an old man named Simeon stops them, takes the baby from Mary's arms, and holds him up as he prays these words:

> "Master, now you are dismissing your servant in peace, according to your word; for my eyes have seen your salvation, which you have prepared in the presence of all peoples, a light for revelation to the Gentiles and for glory to your people Israel." (Luke 2:29–32)

Clearly, Simeon gets who this baby really is! But then we see him turn to Mary and cut her heart with these words: "This child is destined for the falling and the rising of many in Israel, and to be a sign that will be opposed so that the inner thoughts of many will be revealed—and a sword will pierce your own soul too" (Luke 2:34–35).

If you were Mary standing there that day, how would you have heard Simeon's words? Not only would this baby boy be God's salvation, but he would also be a sign that others would speak against in ways that would pierce Mary's soul. Surely all Israel would welcome God's Messiah! Or would they?

At that moment they are interrupted again, this time by an 84-year-old woman named Anna. After being widowed at an early age, she had lived in the temple for more than six decades, fasting and praying that God would act to redeem Israel. Now, standing there with Mary and Joseph, she knows that God is on the march. This child is God's Messiah!

The Bible tells us that Anna was a prophet, so it's not surprising that she immediately began to preach to "all who were looking for the redemption of Jerusalem" (Luke 2:38). Grasping the significance of the baby in Mary's arms, she could praise God and proclaim the salvation godly people in Jerusalem longed to hear.

Scholars often note how Luke pairs a man and a woman in various ways throughout his Gospel. Here we see two old people, Simeon and Anna, independent of one another, accosting Mary and Joseph in the temple. Both understand who this child is. In his response, Simeon prays and then speaks to Mary; but in her response, Anna turns to the crowds milling around the temple and begins to tell all of them the good news: God's Messiah has come!

This is the task of a prophet, as the Apostle Paul tells us in 1 Corinthians 14:3: "Those who prophesy speak to other people for their upbuilding and encouragement and consolation." That was Anna's message to those "who were looking for the redemption of Jerusalem." It was also the message that confirmed for Mary once more that her son was indeed God's Messiah. This built her up, encouraged her, and consoled her.

Anna was a prophet who used every opportunity offered her to proclaim God's message to any who would listen. Whatever our vocation, we can praise God for the gift of salvation through Jesus Christ. But if our vocation allows us room to build up, encourage, or console others, then we also carry out the vocation of a prophet. Anna wisely did so, and so may we.

 Food for Thought

What has God given you (in wisdom or experience) to share with others?

_____

_____

_____

_____

_____

_____

Think of someone whose load you might be able to lift a bit with words of wisdom and insight. How would you go about helping that person?

_____

_____

_____

_____

_____

_____

_____

_____

Prayer

> *Lord,*
>
> *If there is someone in my workplace who needs my encouragement or consolation, help me to be aware and willing to be your spokesperson in that person's life. I shrink from pushing myself forward in this way, but I want to be your instrument of peace where possible. I ask this in Jesus' name.*
>
> *Amen.*

Chapter 2

Three Women Benefactors

Lesson #1: The First Benefactor—Mary Magdalene (Luke 8:1–3)

> [Jesus] went on through cities and villages, proclaiming and bringing the good news of the kingdom of God. The twelve were with him, as well as some women who had been cured of evil spirits and infirmities: Mary, called Magdalene, from whom seven demons had gone out, and Joanna, the wife of Herod's steward Chuza, and Susanna, and many others, who provided for them out of their resources.

Given the patriarchal society of first-century Palestine in which women were often sequestered, have you ever wondered how these women could travel all around Galilee with Jesus and the twelve disciples without creating even a hint of scandal? It's easy to dismiss or overlook our text because it doesn't fit with what we already know about women's lives in Jesus' time and place.

But the reality remains that a group of women were part of Jesus' traveling band, women who had been touched and healed by Jesus at some point in their lives and now committed themselves to seeing after Jesus' physical welfare. The first one named in our text is Mary from the village of Magdala (so Mary Magdalene).

From Luke 8:1–3 we learn three things about Mary Magdalene. First, she had been afflicted by seven demons that made her life a torment. We don't know any details about that affliction, or when or how Jesus drove out the evil spirits. We know only that she had experienced a deliverance that left her wanting nothing more in life than to stay close to her deliverer and serve him however she was able.

The second thing we learn about her from our text is that she was a benefactor of Jesus. This meant that she most likely "came from money." She was part of the Galilean "upper crust." She had resources she could contribute to feeding and caring for Jesus and his twelve male disciples. It was this that made it possible for her and the other women to travel openly with Jesus and his band.

Benefaction in the first century conferred liberties on women who had money and could use it to support groups or communities. Throughout the Roman Empire we find public statues of women benefactors who had aided their towns or cities. While other women might have been confined within the four walls of their homes, women benefactors had the freedom to come and go in public without being censured. Mary Magdalene had resources that allowed her to do what many Jewish women could not: travel freely and without criticism all over Galilee with a band of men, and back and forth to Jerusalem down in Judea for the great Jewish feasts.

The third thing we know about her is that she was a permanent part of Jesus' traveling band. She first appears in our text early in Jesus' earthly ministry, and we meet her again and again in later chapters of all of the four Gospels. She was part of his band on that final journey to Jerusalem. As Jesus was arrested, tried, un-lawfully convicted, and sentenced to death on a Roman cross, she was there (John 19:25). She was among the women who followed his dead body and saw where he was buried (Matt. 27:61). And she was one of the women who carried spices to that tomb as soon as the Sabbath ended so that they could anoint the body properly for burial (Matt. 28:1). *And* she was the one sent by Jesus with the first announcement of his resurrection: "Go to my brothers and say to them, 'I am ascending to my Father and your Father, to my God and your God.' Mary Magdalene went and announced to the disciples, 'I have seen the Lord'" (John 20:17–18). To the end, she was his faithful follower and aide.

Mary Magdalene is mentioned more often (fourteen times) than any other woman in all of the New Testament. When the Gospel writers composed their accounts of Jesus' life and ministry decades after the resurrection, they named Mary Magdalene so often because even then she was well known to Christians throughout the Roman Empire for her service to Jesus.

 Food for Thought

Mary Magdalene experienced deliverance from demonic possession as Jesus healed her. What has Jesus done for you that calls forth your gratitude to him?

_____

_____

_____

_____

_____

_____

_____

Mary Magdalene used what she had (money) to serve Jesus. What do you have that could also serve him?

_____

_____

_____

_____

_____

_____

_____

Lesson #2: The Second Benefactor—Joanna (Luke 8:1–3)

It's fascinating to see how God places people in positions that can benefit the spread of the good news Jesus came to give us. One of these interesting stories is about "Joanna, the wife of Herod's steward, Chuza." We meet her in Luke 8 as one of the many women benefactors of Jesus during his earthly ministry. We can easily slide over women like Joanna mentioned in Luke 8:3, but if we do so we miss an important clue about Jesus' ministry in Galilee.

About Mary we learned that she came from the town of Magdala. Of Joanna we learn that she was married to Chuza, whose day job was as steward or manager to the tetrarch/king, Herod Antipas. So what? How do these details help us? Let's start with the king: Antipas was one of the sons of Herod the Great, upon whose death the kingdom was divided into four parts and given to three of his sons. Herod Antipas inherited Galilee and Perea (two territories separated by the Decapolis between them). His father had been a builder, and Antipas followed his example. He built a new capital, the city of Tiberias, on the western shore of the Sea of Galilee. Soon the town had a stadium, a royal palace, as well as a place of prayer. Pious Jews refused to live there because he built over a graveyard, so he had to bring in a mix of foreigners to populate the town.

New Testament scholar Richard Bauckham tells us that Chuza (Joanna's husband) was a Nabatean (from Northern Arabia) by birth, not a Jew. Antipas's grandmother was Nabatean, and the king himself married the daughter of the Nabatean king Aretas IV to cement a political peace. "The Nabatean kingdom was the foreign power of most importance, after Rome, to the Herods" (Richard Bauckham, *Gospel Women: Studies of the Named Women in the Gospels* [Eerdmans, 2002], 157). Appointing Chuza as a high-ranking official in his court had political advantages. Chuza was Herod's *epitropos* ("steward") but likely much more, possibly in charge of Antipas's properties and revenues.

Because marriages often reflected important alliances, Joanna, daughter of a wealthy Jewish family in Galilee, was married to Chuza. As such, she may have lived in the palace and had access to powerful people. This may account for the freedom Jesus had to minister throughout Galilee without run-ins with officials (in contrast to his experiences in Judea). So her patronage likely had two functions: she had abundant funds to help support Jesus' work, and her position may have kept local antagonists from hindering Jesus' ministry in Galilee.

If you've ever wondered how Jesus and the twelve disciples could have survived for three years of itinerant ministry around Galilee without an income, look no further than to the women in Luke 8:3. These were women who at some time in the past had been healed by Jesus, and they were women with financial means to support his work. Their gratitude to Jesus for releasing them from debilitating illnesses was shown in their willingness to invest their own lives, traveling with him and seeing to all of his needs.

We also can't overlook the contrast between Jesus' freedom to minister in Galilee during those three years and the constant ha-rassment he endured from religious leaders when he was down in Judea. It is possible that God placed Joanna as one of his traveling companions because her influence in the palace could guarantee his freedom of movement in Galilee.

We never know all that God is "engineering" for us as we carry out our work in his name. But we can rest in the reality that often in invisible ways all things are coming together for our benefit under God's good hand.

 Food for Thought

What do you think about the fact that wealthy women were part of Jesus' traveling band in ministry?

How do these women inspire you to use your influence or resources to aid God's kingdom work on earth?

_____

_____

_____

_____

_____

_____

_____

_____

Lesson #3: More Benefactors—Susanna and "Many Others" (Luke 8:1–3)

Who was Susanna and who were the "many others"? Because we
don't have the clues we had for Mary Magdalene (her hometown
and her release from demons) and Joanna (her husband's role
in Herod's palace), we need to dig further. This will take us to
a place we sometimes ignore, thinking that it's not really "Bible
study." But it will give us some further information about women
and work in the New Testament. It will also counter the notion
some have that these women were insignificant because they are
not mentioned in the book of Acts or in the letters of Paul.

Luke 8:1–3 refers to details of Jesus' earthly ministry that oc-
curred sometime between AD 30 and 33. But Luke didn't write
this Gospel until at least AD 59, or perhaps later, sometime after
traveling with the Apostle Paul for parts of Paul's third missionary
journey. Also, Luke, a Gentile traveling with the apostle to the

Gentiles in Greece, wrote both his Gospel and Acts primarily for a friend named Theophilus who may have been a benefactor. So Luke is writing the story of Jesus' earthly ministry in Palestine for a Greek living in a different part of the Roman Empire. So what?

Think of the women we've encountered so far in this study: Elizabeth, Mary, Anna, Mary of Magdala, Joanna, and now Susanna. Why would a Greek, thirty years after the fact, care about the names of the women who traveled with Jesus (along with the twelve disciples)? New Testament scholar Richard Bauckham tells us that "names (apart from those of public figures such as Herod) were usually retained in the Gospel traditions only when the named persons were well-known figures in the early Christian communities" (Bauckham, *Gospel Women*, xxi).

Note that of the twelve disciples (now minus Judas), very few are mentioned by name in Acts and the letters. All of them had received the Great Commission, and all of them most likely became ardent witnesses to the fact of Jesus' resurrection. But where? While the book of Acts begins with the apostles and the women praying together in Jerusalem, and then receiving the Holy Spirit's gifts for ministry, the story immediately focuses almost exclusively on the Apostle Peter, and then later (in chapter 13) shifts to the Apostle Paul. There is a strong tradition (not mentioned in the Bible) that the Apostle Thomas went east to evangelize what is now Kerala state in India. We don't know where most of the other apostles traveled in ministry, but we can be sure they were fully engaged in spreading the gospel somewhere in the known world.

What happened to those women who also received Jesus' commission to "go and tell" of his resurrection, and who were also in that prayer meeting in Jerusalem at the time God's Spirit fell on that band with power? Because they also "had seen the Lord," the risen Christ, they too were sent out apostolically. These women's names were given three decades later because they were well known throughout the new Christian churches in the empire. Why else would Luke name them rather than simply state that "many women provided for Jesus out of their resources"? He named them because of their ongoing prominence among the churches.

Susanna is named because in some way she continued to be a vital and recognized part of the ongoing ministry of evangelism and church planting throughout the Roman Empire. Her work changed. She was no longer providing care for Jesus in his earthly ministry, but she, with the other named women, took on the work of evangelism. Roles change and God's call on our lives can expand as we move into different periods in our lives.

 Food for Thought

What might be significant about the fact that Luke named each of these three women in Luke 8:1–3?

_____

_____

_____

_____

_____

_____

_____

What (if anything) does this mean for you personally? How does this impact the way you see your own life?

_____

_____

_____

_____

_____

_____

_____

_____

Prayer

Lord,

The Luke 8 women used what they had to help Jesus and his work. Help me see how whatever I have in my hand today may be something you can use to further your kingdom on earth. Then help me to use it for your glory.

Amen.

Chapter 3

Jesus and Outsider Women

Lesson #1: The Outcast Samaritan Woman (John 4:1–42)

In chapter 2 of this study, we looked at some high-class women. We now turn to those considered outcasts. Most women in the Bible had to work in some way, but given the patriarchal structures of society, in many cases this work was domestic and "unpaid." And for women who were despised for one reason or another, they often had to carry out that work at inconvenient times and places. This was true of the woman we meet in John 4.

She was a Samaritan. We need to understand how much Jews despised Samaritans to have a sense of just how countercultural Jesus' contact with her was. The province of Samaria lay between Judea in the south and Galilee in the north. In order to avoid any contact with a Samaritan, most Jews traveling between Galilee and Judea would not take the direct route through Samaria, but instead would hike an additional seventeen miles east, cross the Jordan River, hike north through Perea, and then again cross the Jordan into Galilee. This roughly doubled the miles hiked—all to avoid any contact with a Samaritan. That's a measure of the strength of Jews' hatred for Samaritans.

But in John 4:4, we see Jesus choose the direct route north through Samaria where, taking a break at Sychar's well, he encountered this particular Samaritan woman. He could have ignored her, but he did not. Instead, he asked her for a drink of water from the well. No self-respecting Jew would have done that! Double jeopardy:

not only was the cup held by a Samaritan, but she was a woman "with a past." It turned out that she had been married five times, but was now living with a man who was not her husband. There may have been some reasonable explanation for that. Nevertheless, her reality had made her an outcast in her hometown of Sychar. In the eyes of most Jews, this woman had both her ethnicity and her possible lack of moral rectitude against her.

Yet Jesus engaged her in an extended conversation (read John 4:1–26 for that fascinating dialogue!) and brought her to the point of acknowledging that he was, in fact, God's Messiah for Samaritans as well as for Jews. Leaving her water jar with Jesus at the well, she raced into town and gathered up the leading men of the community, saying, "Come and see a man who told me everything I have ever done! He cannot be the Messiah, can he?" (John 4:29). And soon Jesus had a much larger audience. The result? "Many Samaritans from that city believed in him because of the woman's testimony, 'He told me everything I have ever done.' So when the Samaritans came to him, they asked him to stay with them; and he stayed there two days. And many more believed because of his word" (John 4:39–41).

Most women in Sychar made the trek to the well early in the morning when it was still cool, but this woman had to make that trip at noon, in the heat of the day. Her outcast status made her work more difficult. But thanks to that fact, Jesus was able to use their encounter to change not only the woman but many others in the city.

It is often so with us. We may have an inconvenient work situation, but somehow God works in us and through us in that situation in surprising ways. When we enter into conversation with Jesus (through our actions, our thoughts, or our prayers), we may find God changing us and then changing others through us. When this happens, even the drabbest work can be touched with God's glory.

Food for Thought

The woman was in the middle of her work (drawing water from the well) when Jesus encountered her. What does Jesus' decision to go through Samaria (rather than using the roundabout route) tell you about his mission?

_____

_____

_____

_____

_____

_____

Can you imagine ways in which Jesus encounters you in your place of work? What might that look like?

_____

_____

_____

_____

_____

_____

Lesson #2: The Outsider Syrophoenician Woman (Mark 7:24–30)

The Samaritan woman was ethnically mixed: part Jew, part Gentile. The Syrophoenician woman was Gentile through and through, with no understanding of Jewish beliefs. Jesus had just finished an encounter with some Pharisees who had come up from Jerusalem to Galilee, and he needed some down time in a different place.

> From there he set out and went away to the region of Tyre [present-day Lebanon]. He entered a house and did not want anyone to know he was there. Yet he could not escape notice, but a woman whose little daughter had an unclean spirit immediately heard about him, and she came and bowed down at his feet. Now the woman was a Gentile, of Syrophoenician origin. She begged him to cast the demon out of her daughter. He said to her, "Let the children be fed first, for it is not fair to take the children's food and throw it to the dogs." But she answered him, "Sir, even the dogs under the table eat the children's crumbs." Then he said to her, "For saying that, you may go—the demon has left your daughter." So she went home, found the child lying on the bed, and the demon gone. (Mark 7:24–30)

Parenting is work. It's not just a 9-to-5 job; it's often a 24/7 job. The work doubles when a child is dealing with any kind of disability. In our text, this mother had a daughter who "had an unclean spirit." Biblically informed Christian mental health workers are divided on the question of whether first-century demon possession is a form of mental illness or a completely separate spiritual category of oppression. In either case, this mother is beside herself with anxiety and grief for a beloved daughter. Finding some means of healing her daughter was her number-one task.

This mother is Syrophoenician, that is, from the coastal part of ancient Syria, the same territory from which King Ahab took a wife, Jezebel, hundreds of years earlier. While we know Jezebel as the nemesis of the Hebrew prophet Elijah, she was also responsible for introducing Baal worship into Israel. When we meet the Syrophoenician woman in Mark 7, we can assume that she probably worshiped the many gods and goddesses important in Tyre.

The Gospel writer doesn't tell us how the woman heard about Jesus or why she thought he could help her. Instead, we're plunged into the middle of the story as she begged Jesus to cast the demon out of her daughter. Then came an interesting interchange: Jesus (perhaps with a twinkle in his eye) responded to her request by noting that "the children be fed first, for it is not fair to take the children's food and give it to the dogs." In other words, "My mission is to the Jews, not to Gentiles at this point." But note the woman's (paraphrased) rejoinder: "Yes but! Even the puppies under the table eat the crumbs the children drop. Yes, Jesus, I understand that, but you can let a few crumbs drop for us and heal my daughter!" Delighted with her answer, he responded (again, paraphrased), "Woman, great is your faith! Let it be done for you as you wish" (Matt. 15:28).

The Syrophoenician woman was an outsider in a different way from the Samaritan woman at the well. She didn't carry the Samaritan woman's moral baggage, but neither did she have the Samaritan's belief in the one true God in covenant with the Jewish people. Yet when she heard about Jesus, she came to him out of her desperate need, believing that he could do what no one else had been able to do. It was her faith that impressed Jesus and made him respond. As a result, her mothering work would be lessened as her daughter was delivered from the tormenting demon.

Jesus cared about an ethnically foreign woman who was outside his "territory." In Matthew's Gospel, the disciples wanted Jesus to drive this woman away because Jews had no dealings with Gentiles. But Jesus saw her faith and released her daughter from the power of the demon.

Just as Jesus set aside the Samaritan woman's past, so here he set aside this woman's ethnicity as a barrier to faith. Instead, he praised faith wherever he found it. Whatever we face in our workplace (however "demonic" or crushing), Jesus looks for our faith that he is, in fact, pulling all things together in some way that ultimately will be for our blessing.

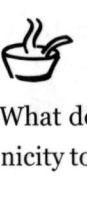 *Food for Thought*

What does this story help us understand about not allowing ethnicity to cause us to discriminate against people unlike ourselves?

_____

_____

_____

_____

_____

_____

_____

_____

When we face discrimination in the workplace, what is the place of faith in how we handle that?

_____

_____

_____

_____

_____

_____

_____

_____

Lesson #3: The Outcast Woman Taken in an Adulterous Act (John 8:2–11)

In John 8 we meet a woman who became an "outsider" by choice, not by birth. She was not a Samaritan or a Syrophoenician woman, but a Jew in Jerusalem. Although she knew better, she chose to act outside the law of her people, and the punishment for that disobedience was death.

Jesus was in the temple teaching the crowds when a great commotion interrupted him. Several men dragged a disheveled woman across the courtyard to where Jesus was sitting. Tossing her down in front of him, they explained,

> "Teacher, this woman was caught in the very act of committing adultery. Now in the law Moses commanded us to stone such women. Now what do you say?" They said this to test him, so that they might have some charge to bring against him. (John 8:4–6)

Understanding that their real motivation had nothing to do with this woman's act and everything to do with getting some trumped-up charge against him so that he could be arrested, Jesus handled their question adroitly. Kneeling down, he began writing in the dust on the courtyard stones. The men kept badgering him for an answer, and finally he stood and said, "Let anyone among you who is without sin be the first to throw a stone at her" (John 8:7). John doesn't tell us what Jesus wrote in the dust that day, but scholars surmise that it could have been the names of her accusers with a list of their own sins. Jesus did not deny that the woman was guilty, but said that only the person completely without sin had a right to throw a stone at her. Then stooping down again, he continued writing as, one by one, her accusers stole away. In essence, he moved the issue from what was "legal" to what was "moral"—the Pharisees' own sinful thoughts and actions.

It's interesting that in the presence of her accusers, Jesus didn't mention the woman's sin. But once they were gone, he turned to her and asked, "'Where are they? Has no one condemned you?' She said, 'No one, sir.' And Jesus said, 'Neither do I condemn you. Go your way, and from now on do not sin again'" (John 8:10–11). Some Christians reading this have criticized Jesus as being "soft on adultery," but the law required the testimony of two or more witnesses, and no one remained to witness against her. In the legal sense, the case was dismissed. But beyond that, Jesus knew that every one of us has a future as well as a past. He gave this woman another opportunity to put her life right.

The Pharisees' work was to uphold every fine point of the Mosaic Law. Jesus' work was to fulfill that law so that it wasn't just about externals but about human hearts and their relationship with God (Matt. 5:17–20). It is well for us to remember this in our own places of work. Legalistic treatment of fellow workers who fall short may be acceptable, even necessary at times. But Jesus reminds us that "unless your righteousness exceeds that of the scribes and Pharisees, you will never enter the kingdom of heaven" (Matt. 5:20).

Righteousness throughout the Bible is about right relationships: we are righteous before God when our relationship to him is right through Jesus Christ, and we're righteous in the workplace when our relationships with fellow workers are right. The whole testimony of the Bible is about how we relate both to God and to others around us. Godly relationships are characterized by humility, gentleness, kindness, patience, and goodness.

Food for Thought

How do you react to Jesus' handling of this tricky situation? What does it tell you about how Jesus may handle "tricky situations" with us?

_____

_____

_____

_____

_____

_____

How would you define "righteousness"? What is your gut reaction to Jesus' statement that "unless your righteousness exceeds that of the scribes and Pharisees [the most religious persons in town!], you will never enter the kingdom of heaven"?

_____

_____

_____

_____

_____

_____

_____

Prayer

Lord,

If I'm an "insider" at work, help me extend compassion and understanding to any "outsiders" there. And if I'm an "outsider," grant me grace to trust you to bring good results from what may at times look like evil actions by "insiders" around me.

Amen

Chapter 4

A Tale of Three Widows

Lesson #1: The Widow of Nain (Luke 7:11–17)

Those of us who live in countries that provide a financial safety net for folks in their old age may not be able to imagine life for many widows in first-century Palestine. In general, here is what they were up against. As women, in most cases they could never hold a job outside the home (so no possibility of independent income). Whatever they brought to their marriage as a dowry or an inheritance was no longer their own to invest or save; it became the property of their husband. Furthermore, in most cases they were engaged to an older man while still in their childhood, and they became that man's wife in their early teens. Because life expectancy was much shorter then, women might be widowed several times as the older husbands died. If they were still young, they might return to their father's house and wait for another marriage to be arranged. (This might have been the case for the Samaritan woman in chapter 3.) If they were too old for that (no longer desirable!), then they were completely dependent on relatives or a son to provide for them. It is for this reason that bearing sons was so vital to women's lives in that time and place. A woman without a son to care for her in her old age was completely without resources.

In the light of that, consider our text:

> [Jesus] went to a town called Nain, and his disciples and a large crowd went with him. As he approached the gate of the town, a man who had died was being carried out. He was his mother's only son, and she was a widow; and with her was a large crowd from

the town. When the Lord saw her, he had compassion for her and said to her, "Do not weep." Then he came forward and touched the bier, and the bearers stood still. And he said, "Young man, I say to you, rise!" The dead man sat up and began to speak, and Jesus gave him to his mother. Fear seized all of them; and they glorified God, saying, "A great prophet has risen among us!" and "God has looked favorably on his people!" (Luke 7:11–16)

Most of us find funerals to be sad events, but it's hard to imagine anything sadder than the future of this poor woman whose only son had died. She had lost her only hope for survival. But Jesus was there, and that made all the difference. In compassion, he restored her son to life and restored her hope for the future.

This Bible study is about women and work in the New Testament. But in this chapter we see the underside of this issue. For some women, social conventions made it impossible for them to work to support themselves. Not everyone has the capacity (either the gifts or the opportunities) to earn a living. For this reason, God's law (given to Moses) frequently referred to the responsibility we all bear to "widows, orphans, and strangers in our midst" (e.g., Deut. 10:17–18). In the Gospels we hear Jesus inveigh against the scribes and Pharisees for "devouring widows' houses" (Matt. 23:14). Later, in Acts 6:1 in the Jerusalem church, "the Hellenists complained against the Hebrews because their widows were being neglected in the daily distribution of food." This injustice had to be addressed at once. So we're not surprised when James tells us that "religion that is pure and undefiled before God, the Father, is this: to care for orphans and widows in their distress, and to keep oneself unstained by the world" (James 1:27).

Throughout the Bible, we are reminded that while those who *can* work *should* work, those of us who have the blessing of work and its rewards have an obligation toward those for whom work is not possible. While Jesus worked a major miracle for the widow in

Nain, sometimes we who work are called to become the miracle that will sustain life for those (around the globe) who have no resources to support themselves.

 Food for Thought

As you think about those in your church or community who cannot work and earn a living, what kinds of things could you and others do on their behalf?

_____

_____

_____

_____

_____

_____

If you have food to eat and a roof over your head, then what are some ways in which you can reach out to "widows and orphans" in other parts of the world who have absolutely nothing?

_____

_____

_____

_____

_____

_____

_____

Lesson #2: A Poverty-Stricken Widow's Generosity (Mark 12:41–44)

How much is "enough"? We all face that question daily, often without thinking about it. When we sit down to a meal, how much food is "enough"? If we go shopping, how many pairs of shoes would be "enough"? How much vacation time from work would be "enough"? If we have a bad surprise when we weigh ourselves on a scale, then it is probably because our "enough" was much too much. So how do we lead the balanced life we're told is best for us?

Sometimes Jesus' math baffles us. We see this in a short story we read in Mark's Gospel:

> [While in the temple in Jerusalem Jesus] sat down opposite the treasury, and watched the crowd putting money into the treasury. Many rich people put in large sums. A poor widow came and put in two small copper coins, which are worth a penny. Then he called his disciples and said to them, "Truly I tell you, this poor widow has put in more than all those who are contributing to the treasury. For all of them have contributed out of their abundance; but she out of her poverty has put in everything she had, all she had to live on." (Mark 12:41–44)

How can two copper coins worth a penny be more than the large offerings of the rich? It's all about proportions. How much is "enough"? Probably most of us would not be willing to consider that we have an abundance. As long as we think we *need* all that we have, we don't have to consider others around us. Once we have an abundance, then we have obligations to share that abundance.

What is it that Jesus is praising in this woman's action? "She out of her poverty has put in everything she had, all she had to live on." This cuts across the grain of all of our self-interest, and it flies in the face of the counsel we receive about making sure we have enough for tomorrow as well as for today. Such counsel is not wrong. Elsewhere in the Bible we're encouraged to be prudent. So when Jesus called his followers' attention to the poor widow, what was his point?

The larger principle here isn't just about money but about what we do with every good gift of God that we enjoy—our talents, our skills, our position, or our influence, as well as our material possessions. All four Gospel writers record Jesus' words when he said, "Those who want to save their life will lose it, and those who lose their life for my sake will find it. For what will it profit them if they gain the whole world but forfeit their life?" (Matt. 16:25–26; Mark 8:35–36; Luke 9:24–25; John 12:25). Once again Jesus confronts us with his upside-down value system, challenging us to take the risk of "losing our life" for his sake.

We might think that all God asks of us is that we read the Bible, pray regularly, and avoid obvious sins. But it's clear from Jesus' interest in this widow's gift that God also cares about how we use everything that we have. In the Sermon on the Mount he made the point that where we place our "treasure" reveals what is in our hearts (Matt. 6:21). That "treasure" isn't just about bank accounts; it's about all of our gifts and influence. In the light of others' needs around us, it's about proportions: how much is "enough" of all that we have?

Food for Thought

We sometimes see how this applies in our personal life, but less in how it applies in our workplace. Where might Jesus' teaching in this story apply in your work?

_____

_____

_____

_____

_____

_____

_____

Coming out of this study, identify some of the ways in which you could be instrumental as an agent of positive change in your workplace.

_____

_____

_____

_____

_____

_____

_____

Lesson #3: The Persistent Widow (Luke 18:1–8)

Justice has a hard time getting a hearing in a bent and broken world. Self-interest trumps it most of the time. It's not easy to see justice prevail over the selfishness of individuals and the power politics of worldly systems.

Christian ethicist Bruce C. Birch defines justice as "the claim to life and participation by all persons in the structures and dealings of the community, especially in equity in the legal system" (*Let Justice Roll Down: The Old Testament, Ethics, and Christian Life* [Westminster John Knox Press, 1991], 259). The purpose of our laws is to provide "equity in the legal system," but all too often people marginalized by race, gender, or class lose out because they lack power or advocates who can defend their cause. We see pieces of this in a story Jesus told his followers about a marginalized woman, a widow, recorded in Luke 18:2–6:

> [Jesus] said, "In a certain city there was a judge who neither feared God nor had respect for people. In that city there was a widow who kept coming to him and saying, 'Grant me justice against my opponent.' For a while he refused; but later he said to himself, 'Though I have no fear of God and no respect for anyone, yet because this widow keeps bothering me, I will grant her justice, so that she may not wear me out by continually coming.'" And the Lord said, "Listen to what the unjust judge says."

Jesus told his listeners that the point of his story was that they should pray and continue to pray without losing heart because God would ultimately vindicate them. This is persistence in prayer. At the same time, we are called repeatedly throughout the Bible, even as we pray, to deal justly with everyone around us (and that includes in the workplace). When Micah asked the rhetorical question, "With what shall I come before the LORD, and bow myself before God on high?" the answer was this: "He has told you, O mortal, what is good; and what does the LORD require of you but to do justice, and to love kindness, and to walk humbly with your God?" (Micah 6:6–8).

There is a "spirituality" that we must avoid, one that allows us to be religious while ignoring the needs of others around us who may need justice in an unjust world. Jesus noted this in his criticism of the religious leaders of his day:

> "Woe to you, scribes and Pharisees, hypocrites! For you tithe mint, dill, and cummin, and have neglected the weightier matters of the law: justice and mercy and faith. It is these you ought to have practiced without neglecting the others. You blind guides! You strain out a gnat but swallow a camel!" (Matt. 23:23–24)

These religious people were so careful about tithing that they even gave God one-tenth of all the herbs in their gardens! But in the same passage we learn that they "devoured widows' houses."

Look around your workplace. Are there unjust situations no one is addressing? Are there folks being trampled under an unjust system of wages, hours, or types of work? This chapter in our Bible study focuses our attention on people who become "invisible" to us, who suffer on the underside of their workplace. When we pray, we are called to include these people in our prayers, and then we are called to work for justice for them. As those who also carry the image of God, they deserve our attention, a voice on their behalf, and even action to correct unjust situations. If we are followers of Jesus Christ, then no one should ever be "dirt under our feet." Our piety is meaningless, even disgusting to God, if we ignore the plight of those around us who need justice. As God said through the Old Testament prophet Amos: "I hate, I despise your festivals, and I take no delight in your solemn assemblies. . . . But let justice roll down like waters, and righteousness like an ever-flowing stream" (Amos 5:21, 24).

 *Food for Thought*

People often think of justice only as *r*etributive—that is, punishment. But the Bible more often presents justice as *di*stributive—that is, sharing justly with those who lack. How would you define the word *justice*?

_____

_____

_____

_____

As you look around your workplace, are there unjust practices that need to be addressed, and if so, how can you go about addressing them?

_____

_____

_____

_____

_____

Prayer

Lord,

Give me eyes to see and a heart that understands the needs of others around me in my workplace. Then give me courage to address those needs in ways that honor your insistence on justice.

Amen.

Chapter 5

When Changing Circumstances Change Vocations

Lesson #1: The Faithful Women Who Watched Jesus Die (Matthew 27:55–56; Mark 15:40–41; Luke 23:49; John 19:25)

As noted in chapter 2, lesson 3, all four New Testament Gospels (Matthew, Mark, Luke, and John) were written several decades after Jesus' earthly ministry. Furthermore, each Gospel was addressed to a particular group of Christians in some part of the Roman Empire. So in their stories of Jesus' earthly ministry, the writers often mentioned by name only the people with whom their readers would be familiar. The name of a person in one Gospel might not necessarily be familiar to every Christian in the empire several decades later. As a result, in the various Gospels we encounter different lists of names for people present at the same event. We see this phenomenon occur with the lists of women at the cross on Good Friday and at the empty tomb on Easter Sunday morning.

Matthew tells us that at the cross "many women were also there. . . . Among them were Mary Magdalene, and Mary the mother of James and Joseph, and the mother of the sons of Zebedee" (27:55–56). Mark tells us that "there were also women looking on from a distance; among them were Mary Magdalene, and Mary the mother of James the younger and of Joses, and Salome" (15:40). Luke merely states that "all his acquaintances, including the women who had followed him from Galilee, stood at a distance, watching these things" (23:49), and John notes that Jesus' mother, "and his mother's sister, Mary the wife of Clopas, and Mary Magdalene" were present (19:25). We see similar differences in the lists of named women at the empty tomb.

Some people take these differences as "proof" of "mistakes" in the Bible, but this fails to take into account the different audiences for whom the Gospels were written. Obviously, Mary Magdalene was well known throughout all of the churches in the empire, so we find her included in every list. Other women were known in some parts of the empire, but not in others. A good writer would not bother to name someone with whom his readers were unfamiliar.

Think for a minute about Acts 2. At least 120 men and women were gathered in an upper room in Jerusalem praying on the day of Pentecost:

> They were all together in one place. And suddenly from heaven there came a sound like the rush of a violent wind, and it filled the entire house where they were sitting. Divided tongues, as of fire, appeared among them, and a tongue rested on each of them. All of them were filled with the Holy Spirit and began to speak in other languages, as the Spirit gave them ability. (Acts 2:1–4)

This happened on a particularly important day, Pentecost. Jerusalem, normally a smallish town of 50,000, swelled to more than 180,000 on each of the three major Jewish feast days as pilgrims came from all parts of the known world (read the list in Acts 2:8–11!). When God empowered that group of Jesus-followers to preach the gospel to the world, he brought the world to Jerusalem. Then from Jerusalem the good news of salvation through Jesus Christ was carried back to every part of the known world.

We can assume that not only the listening pilgrims but also the 120 Spirit-filled Christians speaking God's truth to the pilgrims spread out through the empire as witnesses to Jesus' death and resurrection. Some undoubtedly stayed in Palestine, but others traveled across North Africa or throughout Turkey, Greece, and Rome, or east to India and beyond. When these women's names appear in documents written thirty or forty years after Jesus' crucifixion, scholars tell us that it means these named women were known to those later readers of the four Gospels. We don't know the details, of course, but we can legitimately assume that they continued as active proclaimers of the good news throughout the Roman Empire or beyond.

 Food for Thought

From the evidence of women being named in the narratives of Jesus' earthly life, directed to Christian groups at least three decades after Jesus' ascension to God, what can you assume about their ongoing activities in Jesus' name?

_____

_____

_____

_____

_____

_____

_____

As you think about the book of Acts narrating one part of the church's advance through the Roman Empire, why do you think neither Paul nor Peter in their writings mention these women or most of the twelve disciples by name?

_____

_____

_____

_____

_____

_____

_____

_____

Lesson #2: Women in Transition (Matthew 28:1–7)

Most of us will transition out of one work role into other work roles over the course of a lifetime. We might change vocations, or we might simply move up the ladder in our place of business, giving old tasks to others while assuming new responsibilities (sometimes with a new title). Or we might retire and take on some volunteer work in the place of the paid employment we experienced over the years.

During the three years of his active earthly ministry, Jesus developed his band of followers, teaching them what they would need for future employment, as well as modeling for them the virtues that should accompany their future work. In chapter 2 of this Bible study we met several women who were part of that band. At that point, their "employment" was to provide and care for Jesus in his travels around Galilee and back and forth to Jerusalem in southern Judea. And we meet some of them again at the end of each of the four Gospel accounts of Jesus' life.

Matthew tells us, "After the sabbath, as the first day of the week was dawning, Mary Magdalene and the other Mary went to see the tomb" (28:1). There they encountered two shocks: the tomb was empty (with the large stone rolled away), and a mighty angel (who had terrified the Roman soldiers) told the two women:

> "Do not be afraid; I know that you are looking for Jesus who was crucified. He is not here; for he has been raised, as he said. Come, see the place where he lay. Then go quickly and tell his disciples, 'He has been raised from the dead, and indeed he is going ahead of you to Galilee; there you will see him.'" (Matt. 28:5–7)

Mark names Mary Magdalene, Mary the mother of James, and Salome as the women who went to the tomb; Luke merely mentions the women but does not name them; and John focuses on Mary Magdalene. While the names may vary (for reasons we saw in lesson 1), in every account the women encountered God's angels, and in every account they are given a new task: Go tell the disciples that Jesus is no longer dead but has risen!

When someone died in first-century Palestine, women were assigned to the full preparation of the dead body for burial. But now something had changed: no longer did they need the spices they had prepared for Jesus' dead body. In the hymn-writer's words,

> Death could not keep its prey
> He tore the bars away
> Up from the grave he arose
> with a mighty triumph o'er his foes.

This unprecedented event gave the astonished women a new vocation, a new calling, a new job to do. They were the first to witness the resurrection, and they were tasked with telling the story to Jesus' unbelieving disciples.

The women's faithfulness to carry out their expected work (in the face of the real obstacles of a sealed tomb guarded by Roman soldiers) led to their new vocation. Had they shunned their expected task (preparing a dead body for burial), they would have missed the glory of the angelic encounter, and they would have missed their new vocation assigned to them as witnesses to the resurrection.

We never know what God might ultimately do on our behalf when we are faithful to the tasks we've been assigned. But we can know that God sees our faithfulness and is honored by it.

 Food for Thought

As you think about the contrast between the disciples hiding "for fear of the Jews" and these intrepid women carrying out their work responsibility in the face of "impossible odds," what do you think motivated them to go forward in the face of such obstacles?

_____

_____

_____

_____

_____

_____

_____

Whether in your workplace or elsewhere, what might be any surprising outcomes of your own faithfulness to the tasks you've been assigned?

_____

_____

_____

_____

_____

_____

_____

Lesson #3: Dorcas (Acts 9:36–43)

Some women followers of Jesus Christ transitioned out of more traditional female occupations and became widely known in later decades as proclaimers of God's good news of salvation. Other women remained within their own towns and within their traditional work. We meet one such woman in Acts 9:

> Now in Joppa there was a disciple whose name was Tabitha, which in Greek is Dorcas. She was devoted to good works and acts of charity. At that time she became ill and died. When they had washed her, they laid her in a room upstairs. Since Lydda was near Joppa, the disciples, who heard that Peter was there, sent two men to him with the request, "Please come to us without delay." So Peter got up and went with them; and when he arrived, they took him to the room upstairs. All the widows stood beside him, weeping and showing tunics and other clothing that Dorcas had made while she was with them. Peter put all of them outside, and then he knelt down and prayed. He turned to the body and said, "Tabitha, get up." Then she opened her eyes, and seeing Peter, she

sat up. He gave her his hand and helped her up. Then calling the saints and widows, he showed her to be alive. This became known throughout Joppa, and many believed in the Lord. Meanwhile he stayed in Joppa for some time with a certain Simon, a tanner. (Acts 9:36–43)

We may daydream of accomplishing great exploits for God, but the reality is that most of us will spend our lives working where we are in ways that are anything but spectacular. Dorcas helps us see that there may be glory in the daily grind.

Acts 9:36 tells us that Dorcas was a disciple of Jesus, not one of the Twelve, but a true follower of Jesus living some distance from the centers of his earthly ministry. Whatever she knew of his teaching had led her to use her needle to benefit those in her community who needed her help. In chapter 4 we looked at the problems widows faced in first-century Palestine, and here in Joppa were poor widows and others who needed the bare necessities of life. With her needle, Dorcas was able to meet some of those needs. When she died, because her work was so important to the community, God worked a miracle that brought her back to life to continue her charities.

What gave Dorcas's work such value that she was raised from death in order to continue it? It's possible that some answers to that question might help us evaluate the value of the work we do. For one thing, we see that she did what she knew how to do: she could sew. She didn't attempt to do things outside the scope of her abilities. We might also note that her work benefited the marginalized in her community. Her focus was outward, not inward on her own prosperity. It's also obvious that she carried out her work faithfully, not hampered by whether or not it was pleasant or profitable to herself. In her we see a true follower of Jesus Christ, heeding his teachings and modeling his concern for others in her life work.

We may find it easy to discount the importance of the work we've been given to do, but God alone knows whether or not it has value. Our task is to use our abilities in ways that help any needy people God may bring into our line of vision. This is work that pleases God, whether or not it attracts the attention of the wider world.

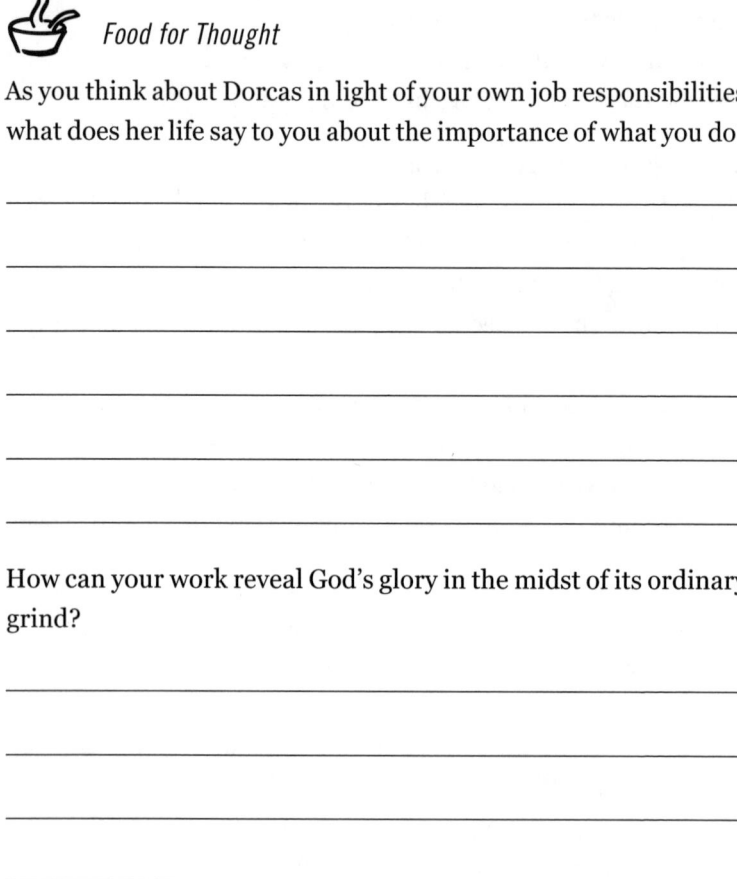 *Food for Thought*

As you think about Dorcas in light of your own job responsibilities, what does her life say to you about the importance of what you do?

_____

_____

_____

_____

_____

_____

How can your work reveal God's glory in the midst of its ordinary grind?

_____

_____

_____

_____

_____

_____

_____

Prayer

Lord,

Some women transition to visible positions in their world, while others remain unknown beyond their local settings. Help me to see the importance of my work regardless of its scope.

Amen.

Chapter 6

Three Businesswomen

Lesson #1: Lydia in Philippi (Acts 16:14–15, 40)

Though she was originally from Thyatira in northwestern Turkey (a town famous for its purple dye), we meet Lydia in Philippi in Macedonia (northern Greece). We learn in Acts 15 that she was a "seller of purple," a businesswoman with high-end merchandise. Any clothing dyed purple denoted a person of wealth or standing because the dye was very expensive. And any vendor of such garments, by virtue of the up-front investment required, would also be a person of means.

Scholars suggest that Lydia likely employed others to do the dyeing and selling; she was the CEO of her enterprise. New Testament scholar Lynn Cohick tells us that in Lydia we meet a woman who was a well-born and prosperous commercial trader.

How did the Apostle Paul encounter Lydia? Luke tells us in these words:

> On the sabbath day we went outside the gate by the river, where we supposed there was a place of prayer; and we sat down and spoke to the women who had gathered there. A certain woman named Lydia, a worshiper of God, was listening to us; she was from the city of Thyatira and a dealer in purple cloth. The Lord opened her heart to listen eagerly to what was said by Paul. When she and her household were baptized, she urged us, saying, "If you have judged me to be faithful to the Lord, come and stay at my home." And she prevailed upon us. (Acts 16:13–15)

It is interesting that the very first convert to Christianity in Greece was a woman, and a woman of means. She was likely what we'd call "upper-middle class" (or higher), someone whose influence could catalyze the spread of the good news. Note that upon her conversion, not only she but everyone in her household was baptized. Also note that she owned a home large enough to take in guests for an extended period of time, as well as to serve as the gathering place for the newly planted church.

Bible scholars point out that no husband is mentioned in the text. Some think she was a widow; others speculate that her husband was away from home on an extended trip for business or for the government. In any event, she was in charge of her household with the freedom to invite the apostles to stay there.

She was also a "God-fearer," or in our text, one who worshiped God. She had already taken a major step away from the pagan Greek and Roman pantheons of quasi-deities. God's Spirit had been at work in her mind and heart so that she was prepared for the apostles' message as soon as she heard it.

Philippi was a Roman city (established in Greece) and the Roman idea of the *paterfamilias* made it next to impossible for anyone in a family to convert if the father did not first do so. But in Lydia we see a woman who hears the word of God, responds to it on her own initiative, and then invites her entire household to put their trust in Jesus Christ and be baptized. As the Apostle Paul's first convert on Greek soil, she had the means and the will to follow Jesus and to put her home and her influence to work so that others could hear the same good news.

Food for Thought

What might be the advantages to the spread of the gospel if people of means become Christians and then use their wealth and influence to that end?

_____

_____

_____

_____

_____

_____

_____

What might be ways in which you have means or influence that God could use to help someone else become a follower of Jesus Christ?

_____

_____

_____

_____

_____

_____

_____

Lesson #2: Damaris in Athens (Acts 17:34)

Let's follow the apostles Paul and Silas after they left Philippi. Their next stop was Thessalonica, the major city of Macedonia, where they preached. The result was that "a great many of the devout Greeks *and not a few of the leading women*" were persuaded and joined Paul and Silas (Acts 17:4; emphasis added). But the apostles' presence and preaching caused an uproar in that city, and to protect the apostles, the new Christians hurried Paul and Silas off to Berea. There Paul and Silas found that "these Jews were more receptive than those in Thessalonica, for they welcomed the message very eagerly and examined the scriptures every day to see whether these things were so. Many of them therefore believed, *including not a few Greek women and men of high standing*" (Acts 17:11–12; emphasis added). When angry Jews in Thessalonica heard that Paul and Silas were preaching with good results in Berea, they sent a delegation there to stir up a riot, so that the apostles again had to leave. Paul ended up in Athens alone.

Did you pick up that many of the "leading women" in Thessalonica and many of the "Greek women and men of high standing" in Berea were among the first to respond to the good news about Jesus? What might have caused that?

We may find a clue from what happened when Paul reached Athens, where "he was deeply distressed to see that the city was full of idols" (Acts 17:16). We watch him argue with Jews in the synagogue and with philosophers in the marketplace every day. At that point he is taken to the Areopagus, a point in the city where orators could be heard by large crowds. Once there, Paul preaches about Jesus and the resurrection:

> "As I went through the city and looked carefully at the objects of your worship, I found among them an altar with the inscription 'to

an unknown god.' What therefore you worship as unknown, this I
proclaim to you. The God who made the world and everything in it,
he who is Lord of heaven and earth, does not live in shrines made
by human hands, nor is he served by human hands, as though
he needed anything, since he himself gives to all mortals life and
breath and all things. . . . For 'in him we live and move and have
our being'; as even some of your own poets have said, 'For we too
are his offspring.'" (Acts 17:23–28)

Note how Paul situated his sermons to his setting and laid out
his argument logically. The "leading women and men" in Thessalonica and Berea had responded to a message that made sense
to them. Now in Athens, while some scoffed, others "joined him
and became believers, including Dionysius the Areopagite and
a woman named Damaris, and others with them" (Acts 17:34).

Once more we meet a named woman who responds to the good
news of Jesus. We don't know what business drew her to the
Areopagus that day, but we do know that she had enough intelli-
gence to follow Paul's logic and then to respond to the message
he brought. The fact that Luke names these two converts among
those who believed Paul's message means that Christians in the
Roman Empire would know not only of their conversion but of the
fruits of their labor for Christ that followed. We would not have
Damaris's name if she had not distinguished herself among the
Christians in Athens following her conversion.

Was she a businesswoman like Lydia? We have no information to
support or deny that. What we do know is that once she became
a believer, she worked faithfully and notably to spread the word
about Jesus in Athens.

Food for Thought

How do you react to the reality that, in hearing the message of Jesus, "some scoffed, but others became believers"? What kinds of things might hold people back from believing?

_____

_____

_____

_____

_____

_____

_____

Conversely, in your opinion, what in the message of Jesus is most compelling?

_____

_____

_____

_____

_____

_____

_____

Lesson #3: Phoebe in Cenchreae (Romans 16:1–2)

From Athens, Paul then went to Corinth, where he settled down for eighteen months, teaching the many new believers in Jesus (Acts 18:1–17). Among them was a businesswoman/benefactor named Phoebe. We meet her at the end of a long letter the apostle wrote to the Christians in the city of Rome. It's likely that she was traveling from Corinth to Rome on business and became the courier of this letter. So Paul needed to introduce her to the Roman Christians:

> I commend to you our sister Phoebe, a deacon of the church at Cenchreae, so that you may welcome her in the Lord as is fitting for the saints, and help her in whatever she may require from you, for she has been a benefactor of many and of myself as well. (Rom. 16:1–2)

Cenchreae was a suburb of the important Greek city, Corinth, and in his eighteen months in that area, Paul had seen a number of house churches emerge. Phoebe was a leader of one of them. We know that from two words Paul uses to describe her.

First, he calls her a *deacon* of the church, a term that he uses for only five people in his letters. He uses it to describe: his own ministry (Eph. 3:7; Col. 1:23), Tychicus (Eph. 6:21; Col. 4:7), Epaphras (Col. 1:7), Timothy (1 Thess. 3:2; 1 Tim. 4:6), and Phoebe (Rom. 16:1). Whatever Paul and his co-workers were doing in their deacon roles, Phoebe must also have been doing. (Note that in the Greek he does not call her a *deaconess* [*diakonessa*] but uses the masculine form used for himself and the three other men.)

Second, he calls her *prostatis* (16:2). Translators often back away from this word, translating it as "a great help" or "a patron of many" or "a benefactor of many." But according to the lexicographer Thayer, the first meaning of the Greek word is "a woman set over others." It's the feminine form of the noun designating a leader. In the early second century, Justin Martyr used the masculine form *prostates* to describe "the president or presiding officer of a local church," one who "preaches, teaches, presides at the Lord's Table." Paul uses a cognate from the same Greek root in Romans 12:8, where the word is translated as *leadership*. In his first letter to the Thessalonians, it is usually translated "are over you, have charge of you" (5:12).

We don't know the specifics of Phoebe's ministry in the church in Cenchreae, but we must be alert to more possibilities than some translations offer. After all, Paul calls her both *deacon* and *prostatis*. Clearly, she was more than just a "helper of others."

Recall from chapter 2 the women who were benefactors to Jesus and his band during his earthly ministry. These were women of means whom Jesus had healed of some disease and who, in turn and in gratitude, used their means to support the Lord's ministry. Now in Phoebe we meet a similar woman, using her position and means in leadership in one of the Corinthian house churches. Women such as Phoebe blow apart some of the ideas many Christians have about women—both those in the first-century Roman Empire and in our world today.

 Food for Thought

What do you now know about Phoebe that you didn't know before?

_____

_____

_____

_____

_____

_____

We now know that women are particularly wired for multitasking. How does Phoebe's involvement in the church mesh with her "secular" work as a businesswoman?

_____

_____

_____

_____

_____

_____

_____

_____

Prayer

Lord,

I work in order to eat and put a roof over my head. I can't give that up. Show me how I can serve you while also being faithful in my job.

Amen.

Chapter 7

Three Ministering Couples

Lesson #1: Philemon and Apphia in Colosse (Philemon)

God designed men and women to work together, each bringing their unique gifts to their common work. We see this in Genesis 1:26–28:

> Then God said, "Let us make humankind in our image, according to our likeness; and let them have dominion over the fish of the sea, and over the birds of the air, and over the cattle, and over all the wild animals of the earth, and over every creeping thing that creeps upon the earth." So God created humankind in his image, in the image of God he created them; male and female he created them. God blessed them, and God said to them, "Be fruitful and multiply, and fill the earth and subdue it; and have dominion over the fish of the sea and over the birds of the air and over every living thing that moves upon the earth."

The Creation Mandate for us as human beings has two parts: parenting and dominion. We understand that to create a child, it takes both a man and a woman, but often we then assign the parenting task to the woman and the dominion task to the man. But that was not God's intention in Genesis 1. Both mandates came to both the man and the woman.

Genesis 1 gives us the telescopic view; Genesis 2 moves us in for a more microscopic view of the mandate. In Genesis 2:18 we find that when God created the woman, he did so as a unique "help" to the man. She was created as the man's *ezer*. It's important

that we understand the importance of this word, usually translated as "helper." In everyday parlance, a helper is a subordinate,
like a plumber's apprentice. But this Hebrew word (appearing
in the Old Testament twenty-one times) is used sixteen times to
describe God as our helper. God is anything but a subordinate;
he is the one who comes to our aid when we're helpless. (Of the
five times the word appears in the Old Testament, it is used twice
here in Genesis 2 regarding the woman. In the other three places,
it refers to a superior army being called in to help the Jews fight
off a more powerful enemy.) Women are created and gifted to be
that *ezer* kind of helper. In the Garden of Eden, the woman was
there for more than simply handing Adam a rake. (For more on
ezer women, see *Women and Work in the Old Testament* in the
Theology of Work Bible and Your Work Study Series.)

When we turn to the New Testament we find women working
alongside the apostles in ministry, and particularly we find some
husband/wife teams engaged in church planting and management.
One such couple often overlooked is found in Paul's short letter to
Philemon: "To Philemon our dear friend and co-worker, to Apphia
our sister, to Archippus our fellow soldier, and to the church in
your house" (Philemon 1–2). Scholars assume that Apphia is Philemon's wife and either the mother or sister of Archippus. In the
first century AD, virtually all groups of Christians met in homes,
and the hosts were the leaders of that church. (Church buildings
for public worship did not appear until the early fourth century
when Christianity was legalized.) Apphia was Philemon's *ezer* in
ministry. From later history, we learn that during the reign of the
Roman emperor Nero, Apphia—along with Philemon, Onesimus,
and Archippus—was stoned to death. Had she not been a leader
in the Colossian church, it's less likely that she would have been
martyred.

 *Food for Thought*

What are the implications (in both the workplace and the home) that God created men and women to work together, each bringing help the other needs?

_____

_____

_____

_____

_____

_____

_____

What are the implications of this for our work in the body of Christ, the church?

_____

_____

_____

_____

_____

_____

_____

_____

Lesson #2: Priscilla and Aquila in Rome, Corinth, and Ephesus (Romans 16:3–4)

Most ministry couples are mentioned only once in the New Testament apostolic letters, but one couple stands out. Priscilla and Aquila are mentioned six times (Acts 18:2, 18, 26; 1 Cor. 16:19; Rom. 16:3–4; 2 Tim. 4:19), and when we follow them around in ministry, we understand why they are such important role models. We meet them first in Corinth:

> Paul left Athens and went to Corinth. There he found a Jew named Aquila, a native of Pontus, who had recently come from Italy with his wife Priscilla, because Claudius had ordered all Jews to leave Rome. Paul went to see them, and, because he was of the same trade, he stayed with them, and they worked together—by trade they were tentmakers. (Acts 18:1–3)

Intermittent persecutions by Roman emperors often forced Christians to move, and driven from Rome, Priscilla and Aquila ended up in the Greek city of Corinth.

Recall that Paul spent eighteen months in that city; then, taking Priscilla and Aquila with him, left them to minister in Ephesus while he went on to Jerusalem (Acts 18:18–22). It was in Ephesus that Priscilla and Aquila met and taught the gifted orator Apollos who "spoke with burning enthusiasm and taught accurately the things concerning Jesus, though he knew only the baptism of John" (18:25). After his time in Jerusalem, Paul returned to Ephesus and preached the word of the Lord there for two years. Priscilla and Aquila were his constant fellow workers.

The persecution of Jews in Rome ended, and at some point this missionary couple returned to the city. We next meet them in Paul's letter to the Christians in the Roman capital: "Greet Prisca and Aquila, who work with me in Christ Jesus, and who risked their necks for my life, to whom not only I give thanks, but also all the churches of the Gentiles. Greet also the church in their house" (Rom. 16:3–5a).

Four of the six times this couple is mentioned in Paul's letters, Priscilla's name comes first. This is unusual, and scholars suggest that she was "the stronger character" (*International Standard Bible Encyclopedia*, vol. 1, edited by Geoffrey W. Bromiley [Eerdmans, 1995], 211). Other scholars point out that while the text is clear that Aquila was a Jew (who had taken a Roman name), Priscilla was likely a Gentile from a prominent Roman family. Archaeologists point to numerous inscriptions and buildings in Rome named for her. If so, she would have been well educated. And if she married the Jew Aquila (possibly a freedman of the Roman senator Aquila Pontius), she would have also learned the Hebrew Bible as a convert to Judaism before hearing the gospel of Jesus Christ. Some scholars over the centuries have suggested that this ministry couple actually authored the letter to the Hebrews. This is a conjecture, but with some solid scholarly support.

What we do know is that after missionary church planting in Corinth and Ephesus, Priscilla and Aquila were back in Rome, leading a church that met in their home. Once more we see a married couple serving God's kingdom as a team, each bringing to their work the unique gifts for ministry that mirrored God's original intention for men and women to work together.

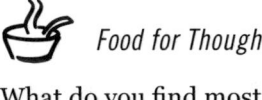 *Food for Thought*

What do you find most striking about Priscilla and Aquila?

_____

_____

_____

_____

_____

What implications for your workplace can you draw from their work?

_____

_____

_____

_____

_____

_____

_____

_____

Lesson #3: Andronicus and Junia (Romans 16:7)

In Romans 16:7 we read, "Greet Andronicus and Junia, my relatives who were in prison with me; they are prominent among the apostles, and they were in Christ before I was." While some Bible translations still retain the erroneous name *Junias* (converting this feminine name into a masculine name), most translators now recognize that here we are most likely dealing with a married couple who traveled about as apostles. The early church fathers (Chrysostom, Origen, and Jerome) all assumed that Junia was a woman. Chrysostom wrote, "O how great is the devotion of this woman that she should be even counted worthy of the appellation of apostle!"

It was Aegidius of Rome (1245–1316) who first referred to Andronicus and Junia as "men," after which churchmen assumed Junia was male. But when scholars search first-century Roman name lists for "Junias," they find nothing. Junia was a common woman's name, and its male counterpart is Junius.

Some scholars have puzzled over Paul's statement that this couple had been believers in Jesus Christ before he was. How could that be? They must have been Jewish. And because they were both called apostles, they both must have seen Jesus Christ during his earthly ministry. But "Junia" and "Andronicus" are such Roman names! Who could fit the couple Paul greets in Romans 16:7?

It turns out that we've already met Junia in these studies. "Junia" is the Roman name for Joanna, the wife of Chuza, Herod Antipas's steward (Luke 8:3). She was one of the healed women who served Jesus during his earthly ministry (see chapter 2). Though she was Jewish, as Chuza's wife she had spent years in Antipas's Roman palace within a Gentile circle of acquaintances. It's not surprising that after Pentecost she should become an ambassador for God's kingdom in Rome.

Some have speculated that "Andronicus" may have been Chuza's Roman name; others think he died and she remarried (not uncommon at that time). In any case, here we meet a remarkable couple who could be called apostles because they had "seen the Lord" before he ascended to God's throne. As apostles they had also endured imprisonment with Paul. We don't know whether their ministry was confined to Rome or whether they had traveled in other parts of the Roman Empire. But it is clear that they were highly respected among the apostles.

As the Apostle Paul moved across the Roman Empire beginning new churches, women as well as men were important co-workers with him. In some cases, married couples traveled together or stayed in one place and planted churches together, mirroring God's Creation Mandate that men and women should work together. When men recognize women as their *ezer* counterpart, God is honored and God's work moves forward with greater vigor.

Food for Thought

When you think of the worker's title of "apostle," what kind of work do you think that entailed?

_____

_____

_____

_____

_____

_____

_____

What advantages can you think of that might come from men and women working together?

_____

_____

_____

_____

_____

_____

_____

_____

Prayer

Lord,

Help me recognize what it means to be an ezer *in the work of ministry. May I see the vital importance of men and women working together for God's glory.*

Amen.

Chapter 8

Women as Fellow Workers with Paul

Lesson #1: Mary, Tryphaena, Tryphosa, and Persis (Romans 16:6, 12)

Recall that the Apostle Paul writes the letter we know as Romans to the Christians in Rome while church planting in Corinth. As far as we know, he hasn't yet been to Rome. But the letter ends with warm greetings to more than two dozen folks in the Roman church whom he knows well. We know that he has worked with some of them in the past: Priscilla and Aquila, and Andronicus and Junia. But he also sends warm greetings to at least twenty-two other people, as well as the families of several others. We may be tempted to think that Paul was a kind of "one-man-show" in evangelism, but this list makes clear that a great many people were engaged in the same work throughout the Roman Empire. He knew them or knew of them sufficiently to praise their work for God's kingdom. And like Joanna/Junia, some may have been co-workers with Paul many years earlier as the young Christian church was beginning in Palestine.

Among those greeted are four women we meet in Romans 16:6 and 12: "Greet Mary, who has worked very hard among you. . . . Greet those workers in the Lord, Tryphaena and Tryphosa. Greet the beloved Persis, who has worked hard in the Lord." Note two facts about these four women: they worked hard, and they worked "in the Lord" (or in ministry). What kind of work do you think they might have been doing? Were they preparing the bread and wine for the Lord's Table? Were they overseeing the church suppers that accompanied the celebration of Jesus' death and resurrection? Of course, these are good possibilities.

But when we study the Greek words Paul uses in this letter to describe these women, we may be forced to broaden the scope of their work. The "hard workers" were *polla ekopiasen*, and the "hard workers in the Lord" were *kopiasas en kurio*. So what? In 1 Timothy 5:17, Paul uses the same word (*kopiontes*) to describe his own ministry of preaching and evangelism. It's possible that these women were also working hard in the ministry of preaching and evangelism.

In 1 Corinthians 16:16 Paul tells the church to submit to two kinds of workers: to those in the ministry of "service" (*diakonian*), represented by Phoebe; and to the "hard workers and fellow workers" (*sunergounti kai kopionti*): Mary, Tryphaena, Tryphosa, and Persis. Whatever the nature of these women's work, it was worthy of honor from the Corinthian Christians who were told to submit to such people.

In his letters Paul calls eleven different people "fellow workers" (the Greek word *sunergon*), a term that always designates those who were prominent in ministry in the churches. These include Philemon (Philemon 1:1), Timothy (1 Thess. 3:2), Aristarchus, Mary, and Justus (Col. 4:11), Titus (2 Cor. 8:23), Urbanus (Rom. 16:9), Euodia and Syntyche (Phil. 4:2–3), and Priscilla and Aquila. Note that four of the eleven are women. We don't know precisely how each one served as a "fellow worker" with Paul, but we can assume that they worked alongside the apostle, doing whatever he was doing in ministry.

Food for Thought

If you were asked what kinds of "work" in the church would be appropriate for women, what would you include in your list?

_____

_____

_____

_____

_____

_____

_____

How would you describe whatever work you're doing that could be called "Christian work"?

_____

_____

_____

_____

_____

_____

_____

Lesson #2: Euodia and Syntyche (Philippians 4:2–3)

Most of us have heard of "church fights," some of which end up in "church splits." This is always sad, but it takes strength to lead in ministry and sometimes that strength rubs up against someone else's strength, creating friction.

Being an active Christian in the first-century Roman Empire took a lot of strength, so we're not surprised when we discover two women leaders in the church at Philippi who were at odds with each other. We read about them in Philippians 4:2–3:

> I urge Euodia and I urge Syntyche to be of the same mind in the Lord. Yes, and I ask you also, my loyal companion, help these women, for they have struggled beside me in the work of the gospel, together with Clement and the rest of my co-workers, whose names are in the book of life.

Here are two women who have "struggled beside [Paul] in the work of the gospel." But they are not "of the same mind in the Lord." Can you imagine that? Of course! So Paul enlists others in the Philippian church to come alongside these two women and help them resolve their differences. Recall from chapter 6, lesson 1 in this study that the Philippian church began with a group of women listening to Paul and Silas talk about Jesus out on the banks of the town's river. Lydia and other women formed the spine of the new church. Without any nearby models of "church" to help them, they had to work together figuring out how to move forward as Christ's "body" in that town. It seems almost inevitable that they would have differing ideas of how the church should be.

It's possible that the apostle had these two women in mind as he wrote his letter to the Philippian church:

> Make my joy complete: be of the same mind, having the same love, being in full accord and of one mind. Do nothing from selfish ambition or conceit, but in humility regard others as better than

yourselves. Let each of you look not to your own interests, but to the interests of others. Let the same mind be in you that was in Christ Jesus, who, though he was in the form of God, did not regard equality with God as something to be exploited, but emptied himself. (Phil. 2:2–7)

The work of ministry is *work* in every sense of the word. And it becomes even harder work because it is communal. We work *together*. This is not ivory-tower individualism, but the hard work of working with co-workers different from ourselves. But God has given us the model to follow, that of our Savior Jesus Christ, who set aside his own interests for our sake. Our redemption would not have been possible had Jesus insisted on his "rights." But he "did not regard equality with God as something to be exploited." Instead, he took the long and hard road to the cross for us and for our salvation.

When we come up against fellow workers wherever we labor, we are called to "do nothing from selfish ambition or conceit," but to "let the same mind be in you that was in Christ Jesus." It's not the easy road, but it's the right road.

 Food for Thought

What difference should Jesus' example make in the way we handle differences in our workplace?

_____

_____

_____

_____

_____

What would be some concrete ways in which we "let the mind of Christ" control how we handle differences with co-workers?

_____

_____

_____

_____

_____

_____

_____

_____

Lesson #3: Overview of Women in the New Testament Churches

Without thinking, we can easily fall into the mode of believing that "work" is what we do away from home between 9:00 a.m. and 5:00 p.m., with some kind of financial gain at regular intervals. But, of course, work is much more life-encompassing than that! As we've worked our way through the New Testament, looking at various women at work, we may have been tempted to think, "Well, what that woman is doing is not really work." But is that accurate?

Throughout the New Testament world, motherhood was the chief work of most women. To deny that motherhood is "work" is to ignore not only the physical demands made on mothers, but also the importance of rearing their children to live worthy God-honoring lives. But not all women become mothers, nor is God's work served only by mothers.

"Work" includes our use of all our gifts. It is work to use our financial means in God-glorifying ways. We see this in the first-century women benefactors, but we also see it in our world today as we use our means for the benefit of others. This is often the primary way in which God's justice is served in a broken society. When we use our means to help those without means, we are working for God's honor in this bent world.

But with or without means, we also work using other gifts. It is work to contribute our creativity to the work of ministry. That includes the use of our minds in forwarding God's program on earth. But it also encompasses all that our hearts bring to God's purposes. We see this in the many ministering women in the New Testament churches. From a tentmaker businesswoman like Priscilla to the apostle Junia, we see women completely dedicated to being God's "hands and feet" wherever they are. We watch them bring all of their gifts into play for God's glory.

Throughout these lessons we've watched women respond to God's love and grace, and then give all they have to respond to the prayer Jesus taught us: "Your kingdom come. Your will be done, on earth as it is in heaven" (Matt. 6:10). That is what our work should be about: somehow, in some way, contributing to the building of God's kingdom where we live.

All of us work—every day. The question is whether the work we do is contributing to the growth of God's kingdom on earth or if its goal has a lesser value.

 *Food for Thought*

As you review your life in the light of the women in these studies, what, if any, changes should you consider making in the use of your gifts and time?

_____

_____

_____

_____

_____

_____

_____

In what ways can you say that you are contributing to building the kingdom of God where you live?

_____

_____

_____

_____

_____

_____

_____

Prayer

   Lord,

> *Take my life and let it be*
> *consecrated, Lord, to Thee.*
> *Take my hands and let them move*
> *at the impulse of Thy love.*
> *Take my will and make it Thine.*
> *It shall be no longer mine.*

I pray this for the sake of your kingdom, Lord.

                        Amen.

Wisdom for Using This Study in the Workplace

Community within the workplace is a good thing, and a Christian community within the workplace is even better. Sensitivity is needed, however, when we get together in the workplace (even a Christian workplace) to enjoy fellowship time together, learn what the Bible has to say about our work, and encourage one another in Jesus' name. When you meet at your place of employment, here are some guidelines to keep in mind:

- Be sensitive to your surroundings. Know your company policy about having such a group on company property. Make sure not to give the impression that this is a secret or exclusive group.

- Be sensitive to time constraints. Don't go over your allotted time. Don't be late to work! Make sure you are a good witness to the others (especially non-Christians) in your workplace by being fully committed to your work during working hours and doing all your work with excellence.

- Be sensitive to the shy or silent members of your group. Encourage everyone in the group and give them a chance to talk.

- Be sensitive to the others by being prepared. Read the Bible study material and Scripture passages and think about your answers to the questions ahead of time.

These Bible studies are based on the Theology of Work biblical commentary. Besides reading the commentary, please visit the Theology of Work website (www.theologyofwork.org) for videos, interviews, and other material on the Bible and your work.

Leader's Guide

Living Word. It is always exciting to start a new group and study. The possibilities of growth and relationship are limitless when we engage with one another and with God's word. Always remember that God's word is "alive and active, sharper than any double-edged sword" (Heb. 4:12) and when you study his word, it should change you.

A Way Has Been Made. Please know you and each person joining your study have been prayed for by people you will probably never meet who share your faith. And remember that "the LORD himself goes before you and will be with you; he will never leave you nor forsake you. Do not be afraid; do not be discouraged" (Deut. 31:8). As a leader, you need to know that truth. Remind yourself of it throughout this study.

Pray. It is always a good idea to pray for your study and those involved weeks before you even begin. It is recommended to pray for yourself as leader, your group members, and the time you are about to spend together. It's no small thing you are about to start and the more you prepare in the Spirit, the better. Apart from Jesus, we can do nothing (John 14:5). Remain in him and "you will bear much fruit" (John 15:5). It's also a good idea to have trusted friends pray and intercede for you and your group as you work through the study.

Spiritual Battle. Like it or not, the Bible teaches that we are in the middle of a spiritual battle. The enemy would like nothing more than for this study to be ineffective. It would be part of his scheme to have group members not show up or engage in any discussion. His victory would be that your group just passes time together going through the motions of a yet another Bible study. You, as a leader, are a threat to the enemy, as it is your desire to lead people down the path of righteousness (as taught in Proverbs). Read Ephesians 6:10–20 and put your armor on.

Scripture. Prepare before your study by reading the selected Scripture verses ahead of time.

Chapters. Each chapter contains approximately three lessons. As you work through the lessons, keep in mind the particular chapter theme in connection with the lessons. These lessons are designed so that you can go through them in thirty minutes each.

Lessons. Each lesson has teaching points with their own discussion questions. This format should keep the participants engaged with the text and one another.

Food for Thought. The questions at the end of the teaching points are there to create discussion and deepen the connection between each person and the content being addressed. You know the people in your group and should feel free to come up with your own questions or adapt the ones provided to best meet the needs of your group. Again, this would require some preparation beforehand.

Opening and Closing Prayers. Sometimes prayer prompts are given before and usually after each lesson. These are just suggestions. You know your group and the needs present, so please feel free to pray accordingly.

Bible Commentary. The Theology of Work series contains a variety of books to help you apply the Scriptures and Christian faith to your work. This Bible study is based on the *Theology of Work Bible Commentary*, examining what the Bible say about work. This commentary is intended to assist those with theological training or interest to conduct in-depth research into passages or books of Scripture.

Video Clips. The Theology of Work website (www.theologyofwork .org) provides good video footage of people from the marketplace highlighting the teaching from all the books of the Bible. It would be great to incorporate some of these videos into your teaching time.

Enjoy your study! Remember that God's word does not return void—ever. It produces fruit and succeeds in whatever way God has intended it to succeed.

> "So shall my word be that goes out from my mouth;
>   it shall not return to me empty,
>   but it shall accomplish that which I purpose,
>   and succeed in the thing for which I sent it." (Isa. 55:11)

"This commentary was written exactly for those of us who aim to integrate our faith and work on a daily basis and is an excellent reminder that God hasn't called the world to go to the church, but has called the Church to go to the world."

BONNIE WURZBACHER
FORMER SENIOR VICE PRESIDENT, THE COCA-COLA COMPANY

HENDRICKSON
PUBLISHERS

THEOLOGY OF WORK   PROJECT

Explore what the Bible has to say about work, book by book.

THE BIBLE AND YOUR WORK
Study Series